T0294248

Selected Poems

Also by Harry Ricketts

Nonfiction
The Unforgiving Minute: A Life of Rudyard Kipling (1999)
How to Live Elsewhere (2004)
How to Catch a Cricket Match (2006)
99 Ways into New Zealand Poetry, with Paula Green (2010)
Strange Meetings: The Lives of the Poets of the Great War (2010)

Fiction
People Like Us: Sketches of Hong Kong (1977)

Poetry
Coming Here (1989)
Coming Under Scrutiny (1989)
How Things Are, with Adrienne Jansen, Meg Campbell and J.C. Sturm (1996)
A Brief History of New Zealand Literature (1996)
13 Ways (1997)
Nothing to Declare: Selected Writings 1977–1997 (1998)
Plunge (2001)
Your Secret Life (2005)
Just Then (2012)
Half Dark (2015)
Winter Eyes (2018)

As editor
One Lady at Wairakei: Rudyard Kipling (1983)
*Talking About Ourselves: Twelve New Zealand Poets in Conversation
    with Harry Ricketts* (1986)
Kipling's Lost World: Kipling's Literary Stories (1989)
Worlds of Katherine Mansfield (1991)
Under Review: A Selection from New Zealand Books 1991–1996,
    with Bill Sewell and Lauris Edmond (1997)
How You Doing?: A Selection of New Zealand Comic and Satiric Verse,
    with Hugh Roberts (1998)
Spirit in a Strange Land: A Selection of New Zealand Spiritual Verse,
    with Paul Morris and Mike Grimshaw (2002)
Spirit Abroad: A Second Selection of New Zealand Spiritual Verse,
    with Paul Morris and Mike Grimshaw (2004)
The Long Trail: Selected Poems, Rudyard Kipling (2004)
The Awa Book of New Zealand Sports Writing (2010)
A Made-Up Place: New Zealand in Young Adult Fiction, with Geoff Miles,
    Anna Jackson, Tatjana Schaefer and Kathryn Walls (2011)
Essential New Zealand Poems: Facing the Empty Page, with James Norcliffe
    and Siobhan Harvey (2014)
How We Remember: New Zealanders and the First World War, with
    Charles Ferrall (2014)
The Penguin Book of New Zealand War Writing, with Gavin McLean (2015)

Harry
Ricketts

Selected
Poems

Victoria University of Wellington Press

VICTORIA UNIVERSITY OF
WELLINGTON
TE HERENGA WAKA

Victoria University of Wellington Press
PO Box 600, Wellington
New Zealand
vup.wgtn.ac.nz

Copyright © Harry Ricketts 2021
First published 2021

This book is copyright. Apart from
any fair dealing for the purpose of private study,
research, criticism or review, as permitted under the
Copyright Act, no part may be reproduced by any
process without the permission of the publishers.
The moral rights of the author have been asserted.

A catalogue record is available at the National Library of New Zealand.

ISBN 9781776564224

Acknowledgements
Grateful thanks to the editors of the following publications and
platforms, in which a number of these poems have appeared:
*Booknotes, Broadsheet, Commonwealth, Dominion Post, Imprint,
Kings Cross Pub Poets, Landfall, Madog, Matrix, Midlands Poetry
Worksheet, New Zealand Books, Other Poetry, Poetry Australia,
The Spinoff*, Radio New Zealand, Radio Hong Kong, Radio Leicester,
Stand, Takahē, Turbine and *Verse*.

Printed in Singapore by Markono Print Media Pte Ltd

for Belinda, Jessie and my mother

Contents

from *Coming Here*

Peking History Lesson (1977)

i

in blues & greens

                talking not looking

cheerful workers

              amble or pedal

through the courtyards of the Forbidden City

under a whitening six o'clock sky

      above each gate

      Mao's portrait

              synthetically benign

      the wart on his chin

      just left of centre

as Lao Tze once wittily remarked

to Confucius: 'times change'

ii

there used to be incense

                  & an ox and incantation

as the priests unrolled

                  the sacred silken scrolls

& the Son of Heaven at the hour appointed

took upon him the sins of his people

      'we must learn from history'

      said the guide with a smile

      as we listened by the wall for an echo

      & watched the workers

      'educated morally, physically and intellectually'

      walk in the sun

      under the curved duck-egg-blue tiles

      discussing perhaps the example of Lei Feng

      who died on the job

      hit by a reversing truck

      fifteen years ago

Tales of Old Hong Kong

She still remembers Hong Kong well.
'Thirty years of fairyland:
the bridge parties, the cherry brandies
at launch picnics. One felt
like a Roman charioteer, water-skiing
in 1926.'

Yes, her household had been large:
No: 1 boy, No: 2 boy, cook,
wash amah, two gardeners,
four rickshawmen, and one
Swiss nanny.

She holds court now amongst buddleia,
box-hedges and phlox.
One hooked and mottled hand
pours tea; the other grips
the ornamental silver top
of a malacca cane, given
by George IV to her great-grandfather.
Now at ninety-seven
she doesn't look a day over eighty.

Wasps hum down the receding afternoon.

'We introduced Brownies out there, of course;
to make them fair to one another.'

She recalls (and with still evident shame)
how at a party of Lady Ho Tung's
a group of subalterns, each of a family
honoured the length and breadth of the Empire,
giggled at the size of their hostess's feet,
so bound and tiny she must have been lame.

But was it dangerous?
'You could say so, yes.
In two or three typhoons I saw
a corrugated iron roof
slice a tree like a blade of grass . . .
And then there were pirates in Bias Bay
who hunted down ferries bound for Canton.
And if they were tried by a British judge,
the pirates laughed – no torture, you see,
like there was in the Chinese courts.'

'I can't begin to tell you
what our womenfolk went through
at the hands of the Japanese in . . .'

While she talks, the afternoon
hardens on the garden-wall;
dead leaves stir in a twist of wind;
the oak tree's shadow re-leases the lawn,
and suddenly I see what I came here for.

The Reading

The audience has been most polite.
And why not? Jacket, short hair, English – I'm safe enough;
my poems won't bite.
I give them a dose of my Hong Kong stuff;
as usual, it goes down all right
(faintly reminds one old lady of Arthur Clough
whom her grandfather knew by sight).

In the second half (a bit drunk) I start to bluff;
tell a risqué story – which falls flat.
The audience is getting bored,
and so am I. I wonder if I were to strip . . .
decide it hasn't come to that.
There are what appear to be two large tusks growing down
    over my upper lip.
I stop. The audience, relieved, applaud.

Aro St

The goddess is a mess tonight.
One lens keeps dropping from her dark glasses.
Her black eye weeps for itself.

We talk of friends who inhabit
ordinary dragon-chasing lives
and now she's mumbling something

about the raven, the virgin and the hag.
'Don't do that, you hear! Why
must you always do that?

Always thinking. The blood blossoms
I tell you. The blood blossoms and buds.
You haven't been there. What do you know?'

And while that dark inward voice
slurs its painful adumbrations
she chuckles as the words hit home.

Te Wairoa: Buried Village (1886/1987)

You turn up here now,
ready for empathy,
but the past resists, insists

on showing you rooms of bygones
and bottles. Look, this one's
full of cloudy champagne.

That cash register's pretty
and so are these stones:
red jasper, obsidian, tumbler-polished.

Hang on. Here's a pair
of muddy shoes (plus laces).
The rusty outline of a cot.

A clock that stopped at twenty to three.
This is more like it. Your nose
bumps against the glass.

Stepping out into stringy rain,
you take refuge in a reconstruction
of Tūhoto Ariki's whare

where he sheltered for four days –
still alive when they dug him out.
The rain unwinds a line of poplars

which they say grew out
of fence posts. Can that really
be true? No more unlikely

that this quick shudder
as the past, unlocked
rushes towards you.

For Pamela Instead of a Phone Call

We'd meant to phone
to thank you (so much) for supper
last Wednesday;
$\qquad\qquad$ kept putting it off
with that faint twinge of guilt
allowed with friends, knowing you'd say:
'No, no. Don't be so silly! Life's too short.'

So when at last
we phoned this morning and the line
as usual was engaged, we felt no
lurching premonition
(you spent your life on the phone). But
you were already dead by then. And now

we can never
ring up and wait for your clear voice
to answer. Thinking of that somehow makes
your death seem real
$\qquad\qquad$ – that and
remembering your face on the pillow:
so pale, relaxed and (forgive me)

slightly yellow.
I kept staring at the blue and
white eiderdown, imagining I saw
it rise and fall – while in my head and out
in the hall, the phone never stopped ringing.

Memo for Horace

They're now imagining the probable effects
of a 'nuclear winter'. Know what I'm talking about?
There isn't time for a lesson in C20th science
but it's the latest explanation
and explains incidentally
why I sit here on this particular spring evening
reading '*Exegi monumentum aere perennius*'.

In this new hypothetical future, you see,
it will not matter what monuments
are 'more durable than bronze'
or 'higher than Pharaoh's pyramids'.
No part of us will survive for long
the 'angry wind', the 'hungry rain':
that last incandescent translation.

Knight Moves

It is not old age nor entropy
        not even cancer
It is not crosses on Calvary
        not even Hiroshima
It is not 'to be or not to be'
        not even your mother

It is boys and girls that you mislaid
        casual cruelties every day
It is the knight moves you should have made
        spaces behind the words you say

Nothing to Declare

Marriage
is   another foreign country
you needn't go to
cannot only visit
but   should you dare
requires entry-permit
money and the whole bit

it has a language
you must learn
will never speak   quite fluently
and knowledge that will make you burn
to see yourself
                    as you are seen to be

it has its exiles   refugees
democrats of domestic bliss
double agents   (indemnities)
betrayals done and undone
                              with a kiss
yes   marriage is
such a foreign country
the whole world   changes
                    upon your entry

Your Secret Life

(for Jessie)

I can see it all already:
sitting up long after the kiwi
and the cat have gone to bed
to do whatever it is they do
when the screen scrambles to noisy snow.

I'll hear you shut the front door
with a soft click that makes me jump –
just time to fix a welcoming smile
before you bound into the kitchen (perhaps
for a drink) blooming with your secret life.

What shall we say? Will I blurt out,
'Do you know what time it is!',
angry with relief that you're home
at last and apparently unharmed
from that film, that party, that lover?

Would that be better or more likely
than a 'Had a nice time, sweetheart?',
poured out with an oh-so-casual cup of tea?
'Sorry, Dad.' 'Yes, Dad.' Not now, not soon,
but sometime it will happen.

Afternoon Tea

we do guilt so well
you could call it a family business

the forgotten lunch-box, the lost sock –
quick! a black hole's opening up

swallow the moment, turn on the telly
something's taken your place

it's helping itself to the honey

Albergo Sole

Lie jet-lagged in Rome in the half-dark.
(Listen to the bells.)
The kids are still fast asleep
unlike the young Americans next door
going pell-mell all night.

Light is already beginning
to lick through the shutters.
(Listen to the bells.)
Was it for this you flew back
across the world? Well, was it?

You're thirty-five; that's the age
for reverting to type or at least
for telling the story so far.
(Listen to the bells.)
They say the truth is

you'll never be other
than the self you are. But it's
all right. The light is
shining bars across the room.
(Just listen to the bells.)

from 14 Found Sonnets Drawn from S(ister) A(ubert), *New and Complete Manual of Maori Conversation (1885)*

1500 Acres of Rich Land

The house, all built with kauri, stands
on slightly rising ground somewhat
apart from the village. We do
not acknowledge that boundary.
The fences have been broken down
by the wind. The plough saves the work
of two horses and a man; it
works like steam. Yes, mortgage is
not a good thing. It is greatly
to be feared, owing to this long
and unusual drought, the late-sown
potato crop will be a failure.
These sheep were brought out from England.
Your dog is devouring my lamb.

Are You Disposed to Enter My Service?

Who was your late master? Your references
certainly seem to be satisfactory.
Have you ever been employed as a shepherd?
Can you milk cows? Can you drive a motor car?
It says here that you have a wife and a daughter
but are you otherwise without encumbrance?
Has your wife ever been a nursemaid? Can she
wash the dishes? Is your wife a good laundress?

What wages do you want? A pound a week? That
is rather much. I will pay you forty pounds a year.
You will have these three rooms and the verandah
to scrub. You will have to do as you are told.

Bring your daughter as a cook. She looks very
nimble. If you like, you can start tomorrow.

I Always Remember You

Are you Miss Celine?

                              Oh! Is it you?

I have come a long way to see you.

                              Warm yourself.

I have heard your father is better.

                              Sit down on the sofa.

I really must be going.

                              You are in a great hurry.

We shall meet again in Taranaki.

                              Give me your hand.

Madam, this is our first meeting.

                              I hope it will not be the last.

I must go.

                              Do not go yet.

How Is It Now?

Do the Maoris wish their children to be educated?
The Maoris manifest an earnest desire
that a knowledge of the English language
should be imparted to their children.
They understand that the future welfare
of their children depends, in a great measure,
upon their progress in European education.
Do the Maoris enjoy great power?
They enjoy exactly the same
electoral privileges as the Europeans.
Are the Maoris friendly with the white people?
We have much cause for thankfulness
in the social and physical relations
of both races to each other.

from *Coming under Scrutiny*

After Glover

In Wellington, in Wellington,
the little critics play;
and one dead novelist was found
in Oriental Bay.

In Wellington, in Wellington,
the cake is very small;
and everyone who wants a crumb
must practise how to crawl.

In Wellington, in Wellington,
the little tyrants play;
and one dead novelist was found
in Oriental Bay.

The Limerick as Epic

Said Milton to Andrew Marvell:
'Writing limericks is all very well;
    but I should have thought
    five lines was too short
for my epic of Heaven and Hell.'

Bene at 13

My son plays D&D all day;
he says it drives the blues away.
I wonder what dragons he must fight,
alone in the dungeons of the night.

Still Life (1976)

everything has dropped

the torso onto the hips
and the baggy grey trousers
you don't wear socks
with your brown shoes
your glasses live on the tip of your nose
your face has slipped like a landslide onto your jaw

your hands are thin and dry
like your one-line wit
that hangs out over your bottom lip
like a butt-end
in the mouth of a ruined millionaire

your brain is a small clockwork owl
curved beak jabbing
backwards and forwards
you're always five sentences
ahead of what you're saying
you know you're as boring as the next man

your jacket is trying to climb off your shoulders
your blue tie is limp
and twisted like your handshake

from *How Things Are*

Separation

What you find with separation
is everyone else had been
predicting it for ages; they just
hadn't got around to letting you know.

Michael for instance leading such
a fast life in New York that you
receive a postcard a year if you're
lucky ('Wish you were here. *Toujours gai.*')

now writes five closely typed pages
proving conclusively that he'd
realised all along the two of you
were incompatible, having slept

with you both. (Thanks, Mike, you weren't
so hot yourself.) And Zoe, who lives
with her brother, a King Charles spaniel,
two blue Persians and three white gerbils,

now says she read it in the stars
the day Robert Graves died, but didn't
feel it was her place to interfere.
I mean, *que será, será, n'est-ce pas?*

Wellington

(for Christina)

'When we were children, we had
red woollen swimsuits, wooden spades
and tin buckets. We sat on the beach,
shouting "Look, Mum, the fairy!"

Oh, I know it looks glamorous:
the sun on the water, the BNZ building
as black as Darth Vader's hangar.
But really it's all so tawdry.

Our first talk was full
of possibilities. Now you hoard
yourself like a Victorian miser.
You're such a coward.

I feel like a leper here
now no one's crazy any more.
I hug my intensity
like some chipped and sullen stone.'

How Things Are

This is how things are:
if you leave their mother
the likelihood is you'll lose your kids.

Of course you love them;
they're the heart of your life.
This is how things are.

Should you stay till they're
older, then go? You know
the likelihood is you'll lose your kids.

You'd write, send presents.
They'd never understand.
This is how things are.

Each day it just gets
worse. Look, you're going under.
The likelihood is you'll lose your kids.

You may or may not
be to blame. It's the same.
This is how things are:
the likelihood is you'll lose your kids.

Under the Radar

Wordsworth knew a thing or two
about suffering: how it's
'permanent, dark and obscure /
And shares the nature of infinity'.

True enough; though he doesn't
mention how little one can
do for oneself – let alone
for others. Always under your radar

and you under mine, we know
the darker frequencies by heart.
Sometimes we seem two ghosts
obscurely haunting each other's lives.

Prep School Days

Sunday is a charcoal-grey suit;
going to Chapel; singing 'Hills
of the North, rejoice!'; hoping
it will be strawberries and Carnation for lunch.

Monday is double German with Mr Green
('Ich weiss nicht was soll es bedeuten');
Bullmore T will cheat at Dover Patrol;
Collard be called a 'little mountebank' in Prep.

Tuesday is waking up to find
pirates and parrots in the dormitory curtains;
Mr John will tickle Simmons P
under the bedclothes before Lights Out.

Wednesday is smoking frosty breath;
potted dates (Synod of Whitby 664);
the headmaster's wife will read *Prester John*;
you will suck sherbet lemons; you will be terrified.

Thursday is an empty tuckbox;
Eagle will arrive but no letters from Hong Kong;
the dead sparrow in the water trough
will have a dead maggot in its eye.

Friday is a bus with lots
of rooms; in one room in the corner
is the whole world; if Lord Scribble
is very good, you will let him ride on the bus.

Saturday is a perfect off-cutter;
Witney will run you out and after your bath
Mr Michael will call you a bad sport.
Sunday will be a charcoal-grey suit.

Luggage

Forty-something, you know
the goods are likely
to be damaged; that's just

how it is. So this battered
suitcase turning up in lost property
with its faded patchwork

of labels from around the world
should come as no surprise.
The lock's rusty; the key sticks.

How much you want to know what's
inside is entirely up to you.

Raumati

The brown sea throws itself
at the beach, reluctantly withdraws;

an ostrich-foot shell plugs an empty
plastic wine-bag; a single claw grips

tangles of leather belt that turn
into strips of kelp, bobbled with scum;

Kāpiti's under a cloud; the wind goes on
rearranging the sand, hanging gulls;

four oystercatchers shoplift the shoreline
as coyly as dowagers in a New World supermarket.

from *A Brief History of
New Zealand Literature*

Bay

The women wave ta-ta to Stan.
Kezia's tickled by Gran.
Florrie the cat
does this and that
and Beryl says no to a man.

Katherine Mansfield

Here

What'll last takes time to foresee.
This moa, now – tall as a tree,
but failed to adapt.
Result: it got zapped.
The trick? Standing upright. (Like me.)

Allen Curnow

Jib-booms and Bobstays

As a lad I was happy as Larry;
now thistledown's all that I carry.
Flowers of the sea
are no use to me;
so why do I pluck them? *sings Harry*

Denis Glover

Mutability: An Ode

There once was this wonderful bay.
As kids, we would swim there all day.
but the bay wasn't real;
it was just an ideal.
Romantic, like Wordsworth. Okay?

James K. Baxter

Nits

Hey Colin, it's just as I feared:
now God's put a louse in my beard.
It seems to be saying
I ought to be praying.
So I do. God laughs. Really *weird*.

James K. Baxter

Psmith's Dream

I know, I'll put Janet and Jim –
and Frank – in a book for a whim.
All the critics will say,
'What a *roman à clef*!
Why aren't we as clever as him?'

C.K. Stead

Quod Est Demonstrandum

Oh fucking's the most awful bore;
it quickly turns into a chore.
There's no need to linger,
just use a finger
and do it yourself on the floor.

Fleur Adcock

Tracks

What's hard about being a bard
is the chant – high, blokey, love-scarred.
It's living the blues,
paying your dues;
who needs to be avant-garde.

Sam Hunt

Untold

The rustlers cross the Rio Grande.
Or not. Judge Dredd draws his ampersand.
A poem's a plant,
la plume de ma tante.
The Kid rounds 'em up in Iceland.

Bill Manhire

Ward

There once was this girl without fear,
liked shells, was a bit of a seer.
She beat up this guy
who abused his son, Si.
After that it goes mystic and queer.

Keri Hulme

Zenske Pesme

I've said it again and again:
the slyest evaders are men.
Their verse, like their cocks,
always reeks of old socks.
It's lucky I've got a sharp pen.

Anne French

from *13 Ways*

Footnote to Larkin

(They fuck you up, your mum and dad.
They may not mean to, but they do.)

To blame it on your mum and dad
and claim it's their fault what you do
takes quite a nerve – as though you had
no part to play in what makes you.

This fucked-up childhood myth's a line
that everyone's at some time used;
it may explain why you're a swine,
but not why you should be excused.

Early Settlers Museum, Dunedin, with Tommy, 1989

eey-ore-eey-ore eey-ore
You chant your new tune all the way
down Great Kings Street. We're off

to the Early Settlers Museum
to see renovated Josephine,
photos of severe beards,

harpoons, blubber pots,
the huge jawbone of a whale.
And for once everything fits:

the bright morning, the lolloping dogs,
the sweet chocolate smells
from the Cadbury factory,

autumn staining the hills.

Swallows and Amazons at War

(for Hugh, Mary, Rachel and John)

Her first collection of poems, *Wild Surmise*,
published by Faber, has almost sold out.
As far as she knows, Roger and Susan
are both alive. He's second engineer on a sub;
she's a nurse, interned in Hong Kong.

Dot's adaptation of *Outlaw of the Broads*,
starring Olivier, has been screening
everywhere to packed houses.
From Bletchley Park, Dick writes enigmatically
there's something he simply has to tell her.

She hasn't seen much of Nancy and Peggy
since their silver at the Munich Olympics.
The last she heard, Peggy had joined the WRENS,
and Nancy was abroad, doing something hush-hush.
That's a joke! What about her languages?

John of course was killed at Dunkirk,
evacuating troops, a posthumous DSC.
In her dreams he still flounders
towards her, mouthing 'if not duffers'.
She wakes up screaming, drowning.

After

Afterwards, say five years afterwards,
you wonder why you stayed so long.
Hope, at first, and the kids; then the wheel
of habit; next, duty; last, fear.

At the time it made some kind of sense,
or seemed to. Now it feels more like
someone else's life whose crazy fairground
mirrors you still know by heart.

The Elephant's Nest Shuffle

It's riddledeedum, riddledeedee,
it's him, her, you, me,
it's the elephant's nest up the rhubarb tree.

It's here, there, this, that,
it's Fitzy's ear, Rutherford's bat,
it's stealing the boots from the pantomime cat.

It's one fine day in the middle of the night,
it's green not red, grey not white,
it's never quite getting the accent right.

It's another blackbird in a pie,
it's trying to tell a line from a lie,
it's on your knees reaching for the sky.

It's deconstructing the flasher's coat,
it's playing the game, playing the goat,
it's the missing name in the suicide note.

It's the broken bit that never fits,
it's young farts, old shits,
it's double or nothing, double or quits.

It's scuzzy rhythm, upfront rhyme,
it's Sally Bowles, Harry Lime,
it's knick-knack paddywhack all the time.

It's the elephant's nest up the rhubarb tree,
it's him, her, you, me,
it's riddledeedum, riddledeedee.

Thirteen Ways of Starting a New Zealand Novel Called *Macrocarpa*

Monterey Cypress (Cupressus Macrocarpa) has dark blue-green foliage without glandular pits; woody cones 1 to 1.5 inches in diameter. It grows 20 to 78 feet tall and 3 to 4 feet in diameter, with dark-brown to light-grey, scaly, ridged bark. In the Monterey Bay region of California this picturesque tree occurs on rocky headlands where it is often misshapen by the buffeting of high winds. Old trees have broad, flat-topped crowns with stout branches. Crowns of young trees growing in sheltered places are narrower, bushy, and pyramidal. This tree is extensively planted as an ornamental, or for a windbreak.
—C. Frank Brockman, *A Field Guide to the Major Native and Introduced Species North of Mexico: Trees of North America*

1. My earliest memory is of lying in my cot, my mother's bright face bending over me, framed in a black aureole by the ornamental macrocarpa.

2. Morning mist drifts above the broad, flat-topped crowns of the macrocarpas like gunsmoke.

3. That March when Wayne returned to the old homestead, he remarked for the first time the way the young macrocarpa cast its narrow, pyramidal shadow across the rotting pink hydrangeas.

4. Wally the Giant Weta was born in a pile of woody cones beside the 78-foot-tall macrocarpa.

5. I do not know much about trees; but I think that the macrocarpa has a dark-blue-green voice.

6. Hidden in the stout branches of the macrocarpa, buffeted by high winds, sat Cheryl, the rabbiter's seventh daughter, biting her knuckles.

7. Beryl clasped the trunk of the macrocarpa, feeling the light-grey scaly bark press against her breast, and wondered if anyone would ever ask her to find his stick.

8. 'Macrocarpa, Monterey Cypress, *Cupressus Macrocarpa*,' mused Inspector Motz that afternoon, recalling Prof Brockman's lectures on arboreal forensics, 'but how to explain the glandular pits in the foliage and could these be connected in any way with the Vegemite stains on Cheryl Alabaster's prize-winning budgie?'

9. Leaning against the knotty strength of a young macrocarpa in the shelter of Granny Hohepa's windbreak, Rangi felt the hot noonday sun beat upon his bare limbs and felt that it was good.

10. 'Women!' spat Bill, kicking vehemently at the pile of woody cones; 'at least you know where you are with a macrocarpa.'

11. The hairs on Colin's neck began to rise; alone on the rocky headland, dusk falling all around him, he had distinctly heard someone whisper his name; the old misshapen macrocarpa couldn't have spoken, could it?

12. 'O macrocarpa!' exclaimed Wayne, beating his forehead against the ridged bark, 'What am I going to do about Cheryl?'

13. 'The white budgie!' screamed Ed, as the moon burst over the horizon and he opened the throttle of his 750cc Norton,

the wind whipping the long, blond hair across his face and he saw with blinding clarity that the way up and the way down were one and the same, a 6 was merely a 9 reversed and Zen backwards was the French for nose and all at once there he was gazing up at Miss Moir's oval face, trying to remember the first person plural of the imperfect subjunctive of *baiser*, and had he known then as he knew now the colour of the sound made by one hand clapping was a dark blue-green, he might never have read *Steppenwolf* and run away to that ashram in Kathmandu and have there been vouchsafed the vision of the white budgie and would not now be rushing towards this consummation with the dark-brown, scaly, ridged bark of the 3-to-4-feet-in-diameter trunk of the rapidly approaching macrocarpa.

from *Nothing to Declare*

The Location

You could do a lot worse than Florence:
all those cypresses haunting the hillsides
just like in a Renaissance painting;
those cool churches full of annunciations
and depositions. What could be more apt?

A July afternoon's a good time.
Bound to be hot, and you will be feeling
so cold inside. And when there's nothing
more to be said that afternoon you're never
going to forget, you can turn

another corner, and there will be
three men (one black) and a woman, standing
by a white deux chevaux that's come off
the road. Watch them stooping, straining, their faces
baffled with sweat, but the car won't budge.

Three Poems for George Fraser (1980)

Polonius: Old Poet

everything seems disconnected

mottled hands mischievous eyes
rough frosted hair and disobedient brown shoes
cheeks with the blush of mulled wine
your soft-vowelled Scottish blur

you shuffle frailly inside your suit
the blood must move so slowly now
your mind still moving in world not realised
you shared the air that Eliot breathed

you know we all tell stories
in coffee-rooms and corridors
ironically envious of your eccentricity
how once you said:
'Which way was I going?
Ah, thank you, that way –
then I have had lunch.'
but Polonius
you are so far out
you're on your own
way back
though it's true you stalk dead minotaurs
in labyrinths where we lack the clue
and Hamlet is dead, Polonius,
and Ophelia too
and maybe you'll never write
all those poems you promised to
you did once live in Elsinore
and for that
　　　　　we envy you

Polonius's Home Truths

'Is there no more to life
than this?' I'd ask. 'Job, house,
kids, wife – domestic bliss?'
'Yes,' he'd reply, 'the pleasures of the eye, nose,
tongue and hand and ear;
these for a time are sure.'

'Has life no more to offer
than this,' I'd ask: 'to age,
to suffer – and then nothingness?'
'Yes,' he'd say; 'words may assuage,
may even change your mind;
but the past – that you may not leave behind.'

What Polonius Said

Polonius said
(he would come most Thursdays;
slow, but dapper always):
'As you get older, the past grows gappier,
riddled with all you've thought and read.'
I'd nod and smile, being younger not older,
but I'm not smiling now that he's dead.

Polonius said
(he would sit over there
on the edge of that chair):
'As you get older, the world grows colder
inside than outside your head.'
I'd nod and smile, being younger not older,
but I'm not smiling now that he's dead.

Polonius said
(he could never get warm,
fingers flexed to the flame):
'As you get older, the mind grows bitter;
love is better when all is said.'
I'd nod and smile, being younger not older,
but I'm not smiling now that he's dead.

from *Plunge*

Plunge

It's all so blue, so far
away, like my father, down there
by the poolside, patiently waiting,

and waiting, for me to plunge.
The water will hurt. My togs
are too big; they're bound

to fall off. I'll come a cropper.
When at last I make a decent splash,
he's no longer around to see it.

The Australians at Worcester, April 1961

(for Jamie)

Gaunt bowling; Graveney batting.
Playing, missing. Playing, missing.

'Dad. Dad, why isn't he hitting
it?' 'Just watch. He's playing

above the ball on purpose, gauging
the pace of the pitch.' Grinning

now, quite reassured, I go on watching.
Gaunt to Graveney: playing, missing.

Your Secret Life 2

(for Jessie)

And now? Now I wait for your call,
hoping a week, two weeks,
isn't too soon. And when it comes
(last night for you, this morning
for me), my heart turns over.

'Dad? Is that you?' Sometimes
there's an echo, and I hear
my own banalities endlessly repeated:
'How you doing? What's the weather like?'
Sometimes the line's clear as a bell,

as though you're only next door
and ten years old, reversing the charges.
Let it go. Now we're discussing
your essay on *Hamlet* (late of course)
both agreeing with half a laugh the play's

really about families, missing parents.
You share fragments of your secret life
(school, parties, friends, lovers). An hour's
passed already. Soon, very soon,
you'll say goodbye, and I'll start waiting.

Free Fall

(for Will)

Twenty years ago you
were born in blood, unfolded
like a parachute.

Now you call from Motueka
in tears. It's raining,
your girlfriend wants to live

day by day, your life's going
nowhere. I try to think
of something comforting,

reassuring: tomorrow's
another day; all relationships
hit rough patches; the thing's

to go with your own flow.
At this last – a phrase
I've picked up from you –

you start to splutter.
and soon we're laughing
at each other hysterically.

Dissolution

You could try the Family Court
in Wellington on a bright, but crisp,
winter's morning and be represented
by Alabaster, Loveridge and Moir, the firm
mentioned by Mansfield in that lost novel.

The judge will probably recognise you
from Miss Grimmett's ballet classes
(the two of you agonised at the back
over your kids' *pliés* and pirouettes)
and ask whether you mind her presiding.

At this point someone with brain damage
and a serious stammer will seem
to take over your lines while you find yourself
vividly recalling episodes of *Perry Mason*
in which it wasn't the chief suspect after all.

And when it's over and you're free
to rejoin the world of mystery and muddle,
don't be surprised if, turning
into Lambton Quay, you hear footsteps
echo behind you, and daren't look back.

Rotoma Days (1994)

A bellbird whistles up the light.
Cecil drifts off for an early dip
while Dick makes tea for anyone

awake enough to drink it.
Garry appears, starving,
makes tomatoes on toast. Emma,

Thomas, Richard and Simon
stumble down, yawning from the dorm.
Belinda, Jane and Robyn

are already deep in books;
Harry's trying to write one.
Max snaps at flies; the long drop stinks.

'Not the same lunch again,' moans Thomas
as ham and salad arrive by magic.
Dick and Garry settle down at 'Lord's'

to shout or groan at every run
or wicket. On the beach Thomas
bowls Richard with a shooter.

Belinda and Harry disappear
along Kawitikaipapa Road
past head-high thistles to the shore

where scarlet pimpernels hide,
and cattle slowly lift their heads
to stare at Simon on a single ski.

A fish jumps in the lake.
Midges bite. Dick groans at 'Lord's'.
Cicadas stitch up the afternoon

till Garry lights the lamps, gins
are poured, Richard turns sausages,
and Jane and Robyn pile the plates.

Cecil wins again at Scrabble;
Thomas does a good charade;
Robyn and Emma don't cheat at cards.

'Goodnight. Goodnight.'
The fire dies down. A morepork calls.
Above the gums it's thick with stars.

The Necessity of Failure

Why this obsession with success,
which gives so brief a glow?
Fading already: won; done it;

past. Afterwards, what then? What next?
With failure, there's so much
more to savour, so much more to feel.

Like a loose tooth, you can jiggle
it any time you like;
the true friend you can never brush off.

Failing is like having children:
you find out stuff about yourself
you'd never known nor dared to guess.

And think of the variety.
There are so many ways
to fail. Not just the smart disasters

like going bust or off your head,
betraying those you love
or knowingly blowing your talent –

only a few of us can be
that chic. Don't be choosy.
Any flop will reward you with guilt,

remorse, embarrassment and shame,
whose every nuance
you can endlessly replay, retaste.

Even quite a tiny failure
can last you a lifetime:
that thing you said, that moment you missed,

will twist in time until you see
how it led to all that
and all of this. Some revelation.

So don't begrudge your blunders,
screw-ups, A minor blues.
Nothing's wasted; failure makes sense.

Lost things

'Working your testicles to the rim'
is not an expression you hear much nowadays;
nor do you often meet someone who says:
'Evensong reminds me of Barbara Pym.'

The Lecture 2

Hooked nose, holed jeans,
he's lounged through Modern Poetry,
said nothing, written less,
is sure to fail.

One lecture (on early Yeats?)
he seemed to be making some progress
with a strawberry blonde
in the back row.

Now, it's the final class.
As usual, I ask for feedback,
comments, suggestions,
ask how it went.

Just as we're about to finish,
his hand goes up.
Silence stuns the room.
'Well, Wayne?' I say.

His voice is slow, infinitely remote:
'This course was less of a drag
than I'd thought it'd be –
and so were you.'

Smiles break out, some mild applause.
Wayne hasn't finished.
'The course was okay. Even you were okay.
But anyway who cares?'

Nice

Why do you always have to be
so damn tolerant,
so bloody accepting?
It's not natural.

If you'd only shout, throw
a wobbly once in a while.
But, oh no, you're so fucking nice
it makes everyone sick.

After Martial

Hi, and congratulations. Buying
this modestly priced volume
of poems shows your good taste. (Browsers,

you're welcome, too, though if you're hoping
to pull that dreamy girl/boy
in the corner, try James's latest.)

You'll find every care has been taken
to include only your kind
of poem: hip confessional,

apolitical, clever, of course,
but not as clever as you.
You'll especially appreciate

the almost total absence of words
like 'love', 'fart', 'smegma' and 'dwang'.
Nor will you be expected to spot

deft shifts in the metre. No need here
to fear alliteration;
protection from rhyme is guaranteed.

For Lauris

We'd just come out of some play
at Bats, agreeing it was like
Pinter on speed:

characters who may
or may not know each other
coming into rooms, shouting

and invading space. Feeling
something was needed to complete
the evening, we walked along

to that café by the Embassy.
The young man behind the counter
looked at you closely.

'You're someone famous, aren't you?'
he blurted out, half-accusingly.
'I know, you're Janet Frame.'

You smiled, went to sit down;
by the time I brought the coffees over,
you were giggling uncontrollably.

from *Your Secret Life*

Epitaph for an old cricketer

Death's sharp off-cutter
has bowled you through the gate.

Then

(for Andrew)

Then there are those who still
can't accept or believe it. I mean,
you were so fond of the kids
the two of you (that at least was true),
so happy together.

Susie, for instance. Sure
you were the model couple, she fought
to catch that bouquet (lilies?)
thrown high in the sun; but now blames you
that she's still all alone.

Or Martin. He's never
gotten over it. He rings, he emails,
he won't let it go. Was it
background, he wonders, boredom or bed?
What was it you wanted?

What indeed? Love, I suppose,
though, looking back, it sounds so naive.
And to grow up – whatever
that means. And then just to shoot out the lights,
go dancing in the dark.

Evasion Theory

(for Anne)

We're always being told we should face
up to our fears, relive that strangled
childhood, that marriage; told that if we
exorcise our demons, we'll receive
our very own happy ending. Isn't
that how the story goes? But read on.

You'll find several chapters you missed.
'Evasion theory', for example,
which opens: 'It's okay to evade
what makes you afraid. Confronting your
fear doesn't make it disappear, just gives
it freer rein. Remember, nightmares

love daylight too.' Next you're encouraged
to consider Oedipus. Shouldn't he
have left things alone? After all, hadn't he
rubbed along well enough with Jocasta
and the kids? And he was king. But, no;
he had to consult the oracle.

So my advice is: ignore the urge
to rummage in your backpack, to un-
earth all that stuff you've contrived to live with;
once out, those furious fears will
visit any hour they like. Keep mum;
bury the dead; let it all flash by.

Old-fashioned Love

Nights are cold, hard as the stars.
I wonder whom you dazzle now.

Modern Love

'Well, I don't know, I think they were
kind of meant for each other in a way.'

The Dead

(for Bill)

The dead have just got clear of us,
that's all; wriggled away
into themselves forever.

However hard we try to haunt them,
we can't, though we can, and do,
put them up in some hellish

or heavenly motel and imagine
they're being rewarded for all that pain,
that joy they gave us,

hoping that we'll meet again etc.
But the dead don't want our company;
it's no use to them now.

We're the ones who carry on,
sighing and smiling in the dark.
The dead have just gone clear.

Haumoana Triptych

1

The signpost simply says: Libraries.
The Libraries of Haumoana:

how grand that sounds;
what a ring to it!

The Libraries of Haumoana.
It could be the title

of some lost story by Borges
or poem by Wallace Stevens.

2

In these photos Richard's
and Angie's kids are still
fishing or playing cricket,

Jade still guards the darkening
beach, the driftwood fire still
glows though you can't quite catch

those foil-wrapped potatoes
that were so delicious.
The clotted-cream evening sky

comes out well as does
that distant boa of smoke
from the fertiliser

factory. And somewhere
out of shot the wine goes round
and Maggie's daughter giggles

and says to her friend:
'Want to see my mum drunk?
It's not a pretty sight.'

3
This evening the white-faced heron
does his silly walk as usual,
stepping so extravagantly,
so daintily, over the mudflats,
through the lowtide water.
But there's nothing remotely
silly about the way his bill
suddenly, unerringly strikes home.

Basilica of St Anthony, Padua

(O St Anthony, holy St Anthony, finder of lost things . . .)

1

Sharp, grey
January morning.
Inside it's dim,
a huge shell.

Prayers rise,
fall, at the high altar,
baffling
the silence.

2

Around St Anthony's
sumptuous tomb
hang hundreds and hundreds

of silver-framed photos
of those the saint
has quite recently succoured,

like Maria (2),
and Pietro (25) – who
miraculously survived

that motorbike smash
in 1956. From behind
one entire glinting wall

a priest, whistling softly,
magically produces
a ladder.

3
In a case
in the reliquary
are the remains

of St Anthony's habit,
brown and very holey.
Higher up, behind the blank

stare of cupid-angels,
budding with acorns,
are his teeth,

tongue, and vocal cords.
The teeth are distinctly yellow
and could do with a good clean.

4
Not to be missed
on the opposite wall
is a most 'lively
crucifixion'.

The crowd bustles
about the cross,
dicing soldiers
concentrate intently

on their game.
Mary swoons.
The spears of those horsemen
must be just about

to prick the bums
of those agonised
angels, while,
lower down

to the left,
a disinterested pooch
is slowly sidling
out of the scene.

Lower Broadheath

There's no Upper Broadheath,
of course. Elgar was born here;
that's the place's claim to fame.

On this lawn I tried to bowl
as fast as Freddie Trueman. This hedgerow,
they say, is a thousand years old.

Today the kids and I swordfight
our way through bamboo, bramble,
tussocky grass, gathering

holly and pricking ourselves
excitedly. Then we string up
a swing in the old pear tree.

Fast, high pigeons; low, slow
crows. A lemon meringue sky.
Right on cue the Hunt clumps past.

Bateman's (1975)

Down the enlarged rabbit-hole of a lane,
past the donkeys into the car park;
the chimneys of the Jacobean house;
the gloomy hallway you worked into 'They';
up to your study – brown and bookcased,
desk, globe, pen tray – just as you left it.

Your portraits show you latterly
as a propertied Alf Garnett.

Visitors just adore
the kempt garden, smooth lawns;
mill, river, hill and forge
for Puck and the children;
this arbour pleached like your stories;
and, as the green fields
fold into the heat-haze,
they drink tea and smile
at that quaint warning
you carved on the sundial:

'later than you think'.

A Few Tips for Immigrants, 1981

1
Best to land in June,
a Saturday or Sunday
afternoon for choice;

that way, jet-lagged, sprayed,
when asked (as you will be) how
you like New Zealand

you can honestly
say that it looks beautiful,
but seems to be shut.

2
It is important to realise
you're now in a Fleur Adcock poem

in reverse; that, unsettled by kōwhai,
wooden houses, light which peels your eyes,

you must switch off your irony, work
on those tell-tale vowels: *pin. pun.* Better.

Now what about that greeting? No, not
hullo. G'day. Don't you want to fit in?

And, for goodness sake, remember: lift
your voice at the end of the sentence.

3
stop the tour

the treaty is a fraud

US has Ronald Reagan
Johnny Cash Bob Hope
NZ has Rob Muldoon
no cash no hope

blue yellow red
stencilled sprayed scrawled
there will be graffiti
cryptic runes
secretly self-evident

4
One night you will wake up.
The earth will be moving,
the bed shaking itself
to pieces. Sorry,

this is not the best sex
you've ever had, merely
a mild earthquake – a four,
five. Not the big one.

Another night you'll wake
to fire engines clanging
across the gully, shouts,
flames eating the sky.

Welcome. Have a nice day.

from *Just Then*

In camera, 1972

In this snapshot it's always spring.
She and I look up, smiling
at someone or something now forgotten,
lying androgynously idle on the lawn
beside faded sandstone walls, our faces
bright in April sunlight.

Then memory jumps to a night
in May when in the dark room
of a kiss she and I blow
up the negative of this
idyll of an April day.

What gives another turn to the screw
is you, the invisible photographer,
who loved her like a shooting star.

El Prado

A damp morning, just a touch nippy
for January. You're here
in this indoor meadow, this art-house barn,
randy for epiphany,
or at least hoping to be surprised.

So Raphael's *Transfiguration*
is certainly dramatic –
in fact, quite literally uplifting.
So why does that boy a-goggle
at Christ levitating leave you cold?

Thirty-five years ago with a head
full of *Gormenghast, Seventh
Seal, Crow*, the Velvet Underground, you'd have found
El Greco's silver-lit e-
longations 'really weird', but not now.

Now what hits home is *Saint Barbara*
by Parmigianino,
a left profile. Her face shines with youth.
Braided, brown hair hangs on her
right shoulder. She's holding – what? – a part

of the tower daddy'll shut her up in.
Her upper lip curves over
slightly. She wears rather a chic pink
number, such an inward look.
She knows exactly what lies ahead.

And here, opposite Van der Velden's
flesh-heavy *Deposition*,
Robert Campin's *Annunciation*.

Mary's a blonde, long, straight hair,
bit plump. A nice girl lost in a book

and apparently quite unaware
of the heavenly rays round
her head, beamed down from top left,
or Gabriel patiently
kneeling, wings half-furled, with some pretty big news.

Talking in Cars

The back road into Worcester,
April. Green hedges, cricket,
the Glover's Needle pricking
the sky. 'Anything you'd like
to know?' asks Father, turning
left at Crown East, his eyes tight
on the road. Anything you'd
like to know? *Yes, every-*
thing. Do you have to be in
love? How do you start? Is
it like in The Lion of Sparta?
Do girls, like boys, give hints?
What goes where? Questions quicken,
catch fire in kingfisher air.
'No, thanks,' you say, as we press on into Dines Green.

Quarantine Island

(for Helen and Marc on their wedding)

Love is and is not the point.
With this high wind filling your sails,
world turns strange and yet the same.

Your craft must be delicate, also tough.
You head for open, unplumbed seas.
Love is and is not the point.

These charts you've packed are full of blanks,
bluffs and sounds you must rename.
World turns strange and yet the same.

Tempests, typhoons, the taniwha stowed away
in the hold: all can be weathered.
Love is and is not the point.

There will be days of sudden calm,
nights when stars burn into your head.
World turns strange and yet the same.

The unknown calls. The day is yours.
Hope and trust will take you far.
Love is and is not the point.
World turns strange and yet the same.

Phoenix Foundation

(for Will)

'En-tnt': that was what you used to call
an elephant. You'd say 'I carry
you' when you wanted to be picked up.

Each time we read that page in *Peter
and Jane* where the farmer is getting
ready for work, you'd shout out 'Boots on!'

because on walks you wore your red boots.
You had long yellow curls like Little
Lord Fauntleroy, a Leicester accent

thick and ruddy like the local cheese.
Once in the grocer's in Stoneygate,
an old lady bent down, stroked your hair,

murmured: 'What a very pretty boy.'
'Fook off!' you said, staring at your boots.
She jerked her hand away as though stung.

Years after, I see you running round
and round a room, arms flapping wildly.
You stop. 'I *can't* fly,' you say, surprised.

But here tonight you're standing stage right
behind your barricade of drums. Shaved
head, black singlet, sticks raised, you might be

the sorcerer's latest apprentice.
The guitars kick in, the blue light spins,
your hands begin to fly.

Glowing illuminations

It's winter and snowing. Your father, who's not your father, opens the door. He's wearing a dinner jacket and cummerbund. There's a party in full swing. Laughter. In a corner of the hall stands a basket full of brown eggs. Going downstairs to the basement that isn't there, you find yourself in a room. The door disappears. You have a clue, 'glowing illuminations', and you notice a picture glowing on the wall called *L'Allumeuse*. At once the walls shimmer, dissolve. In the next room, you have a companion, a girl. The door disappears. You notice the pictures on the walls are glowing greenishly. At once the walls shimmer, dissolve. In the next room, a woman sits up in bed holding a child. A balding man, black hairs showing through his white vest, is saying that other people have done it or had it done to them at parties. You realise that she's a virgin but the child is hers.

Arty Bees: quality pre-loved books, bought, sold and exchanged

But did Anne Falkner pre-love that copy
of *The Princess and the Goblin*
(silvery-blue hardback, Seagull Library

series) which I recently bought
for $8? The flowery bookplate
says: '3rd Prize Attendance, 1957'.

3rd prize for Attendance? How many
prizes for Attendance did they award?
And were they really that desperate

to give Anne a prize? Did someone
in the common room just happen
to remark one today: 'You know Anne

Falkner in 4b, with the bad skin
and the oily hair; she's been looking
a bit peaky lately, down in the dumps.

Do you think a prize would cheer her up?
I know, what about 3rd Prize
for Attendance?' And they all agreed.

Or was Anne 4b's mascot, a sunbeam
of a girl, beloved by all; not exactly
the brightest crayon in the box,

but so friendly and helpful
that 'Surely we can find some sort
of prize for Anne?' What, come to that,

were 1st and 2nd Prizes for Attendance?
Alice in Wonderland and *The Water Babies*?
Or something more up to date like Antonia

Forest's *Autumn Term* or C S Lewis's
The Silver Chair? (No, too scary.)
And, Anne, *did* you love *The Princess*

and the Goblin? *Did* you, Anne?
If so, would you like to explain
why pages 19 and 20 are missing?

And what those red scrawls
and scribbles across the illustrations
on pages 105 and 118 portend?

And the pink, sugary deposits
on pages 126 and 127? Or were they the work
of your younger brother Richie

(the one later expelled from Nelson College)?
And, Anne, I want to know what you thought
of the rum story I've just reread

about grandmothers spinning in towers
whom only princesses can see
and how the best way to deal with goblins

is to make up rhymes and stamp
on their feet. I mean, you knew
that anyway. That's obvious, right?

But now I imagine you clearing up
before the final move your children
insist on, imagine you with other

things on your mind than princesses
and goblins, and though you really
did love this silvery-blue book

with its funny bookplate (it was a joke
– everyone knew you wagged classes
at school), it too will have to go.

Understudy

From eleven to twenty
I tried to be you.

Every day provided fresh copy.
I took a cast of your footprints,

practised your walk, expressions,
gestures, some pet phrase:

'This poem (film, coffee)
is *deeply* bad.' It took me weeks

to catch that exact flick
of the voice, that tonal shaping.

You noticed of course. It's okay,
I heard you say to yourself, just how

we grow, borrowing from family,
friends: normal, like shaking hands.

You knew it was different though.
You could see my face in the water, askew.

Wendy Cope in Newtown, Sydney

To Egg reads the inscription
in this second-hand copy
of *Making Cocoa for Kingsley Amis*,

eight dollars. *To Egg*, it reads,
new line, *Special Reference*
to Pg 42, new line, *All my love*,

new line, *Hugh*. Written in black
biro – a Greek 'a', German
'9', dated *24/6/93*.

Of course, wouldn't you?, I turn straight
to page forty-two (answer
to life, the universe and everything).

The poem is 'Manifesto',
one of Cope's villanelles, sweet-
bitter, for a change. 'I'll work, for there's new

purpose in my art'; 'And write
the poems that will win your heart':
those are the two refrains. Egg, what I'd like

to know is: was it you who
sold this book? And if so, why?
Did Hugh not write the poems? Or did you just

not think them any good? (Cope's
stiff competition.) Or did
their art really 'win your heart', but later

you found 'The truest poetry
is the most feigning', and Hugh,
who'd seemed so talented, so true, was two-

timing you with Audrey, that
quiet girl in Summerhill?
After all, Egg, Cope's said again and a-

gain, with special reference
to line one, page thirty-nine:
'There are so many kinds of awful men.'

Flannelled fools

A name, a smell, some trick of the light
teleports you back to that first evening,
awkward in collar stud and blue tie,
scared and sick. 'A fish out of water':
that's what Macksey called you.

Now you're dawdling off to the nets,
late from a rehearsal. A line spins
over in your head: 'Poor lady, she were
better love a dream.' You realise you're
the one McCleod has a crush on.

Someone somewhere is playing
'Like a Rolling Stone', full volume.
Up at the observatory, smoking,
the stars are keyholes to another world.
Who put the cow in the Murray Rears?

'If Shakespeare hadn't killed Cordelia,'
James begins his essay, 'it would have been
the greatest act of dramatic cowardice since Aeschylus.'
Curtis serves tea without sugar, shows you
his bloodstained Shakespeare, calls you 'm'deah'.

Brandon St

(for Bill)

It's hard to think of you
as late; you were always
so punctual. Here you come

now, turning into Brandon St,
looking purposeful,
your briefcase under your arm.

In a moment, you'll say hullo,
go and order a sandwich,
a ginger beer, perhaps a ginger

crunch, before pulling up
one of those rickety chairs.
Then, as usual, we'll begin.

Dear Nigel, 10 things I never got to say to you

1. that you were my oldest friend

2. that I deeply envied your French accent when Monty Herring made us read aloud from *Tartuffe* and *Les Mouches*

3. that whenever I hear Allegri's 'Miserere mei, Deus', it's summer 1973 at Long Orchard Farm

4. that your half-snort just before you said something wry or ironic lit up the world

5. that I'll never forget your mild shame when you confessed you'd cheated in the Common Entrance geometry paper – or was it algebra?

6. that a quick hug last September outside your local pizza joint in Shepherds Bush was a quite unsatisfactory way to say goodbye

7. that you were surprisingly good at tennis

8. that I did eventually get over the glee with which, out of the blue, you'd mock-innocently ask 'Do you shoot?', recalling that moment at school I put the same fatuous question to you

9. that, after our fathers died, it was you saying 'Now we're in the front line' that made me realise we were grown up whether we liked it or not

10. that I still have your copy of *Pride and Prejudice* and I intend to keep it

Do you still?

Do you still listen
to *Atom Heart Mother*,
Hangman's Beautiful Daughter?

Do you still only
drink half of your endless
cups of black coffee?

Do you still look up
under your eyes, when you say:
'It's not working, is it?'

Do you still kickstart
your legs that way
when you slip into sleep?

At the Getty

(for Brian)

In the half-dark of the Getty,
I peer through glass at Books of Hours,
those late medieval bestsellers.

Calendars, annunciations,
saints and sinners, devotional
aids, dim indecipherable texts.

St Ursula is quite charming
in grisaille, flecked with gold. Saint Luke,
a serious beard, writes, fathoms deep;

there's an ox in the corridor.
And this is the naughty boys' room.
A pair of foppish youths ride a goat,

fingering its horns. David, harp
put aside, hand on bare chest, says
how sorry he is not only for

bonking Bathsheba but, even worse,
for sending Uriah to the Front.
Two shapely bare bottoms frame his remorse.

Then, in a corner, a stained glass
crucifixion, South Netherlands,
1490s. There's a double

skull beneath the cross. Mary stands
to the left, folded in, mouth turned
down. Behind her, a lemon-white sky,

bushy trees, a turreted town.
But it's the figure on the right
who stops me dead. The slightly curled

brown hair, hollow look, mouth agape
could – this sounds mad, I know – be you.
Not the you I so fondly recall

in some bar off the Piazza
Navona, wryly reflecting
on lost boys, and love gone wrong again,

but the you I glimpsed one Christmas
Eve in St Paul's-within-the walls,
swinging the censer, eyes wide shut.

from *Half Dark*

The Frick comes to Lake Rotoma

Fists of wind tug at the flax
a tūī winches up, white ruff,
intent. Shadows flicker on the pines.

Inside it's hot, still; time slows.
These postcards before you are meant
to bring back the Frick, that sumptuous

room, Fragonard's *Four Stages
of Love*: meeting, pursuit, lover
crowned, love letters – all those pink roses,

that jaunty parasol. No,
you're still here, sweat trickling over
your ribs. They knew love wasn't that easy.

Move on through. Pause. Here Holbein's
Thomases, More and Cromwell, stare
at each other across the fireplace.

(Saint Jerome hovers above,
hollow-cheeked, a long fore-finger
in his translation of the Bible.)

Cromwell has a beefsteak face,
double chin, a medieval tough
prepared to do whatever it takes.

More will be no match for him
with his plush dark-red velvet sleeves
which, according to the audio,

'make you go weak at the knees'.
But poised face, five o'clock shadow,
somewhat grim, he's the man with the eyes.

Love and power. Henry Frick
certainly knew about power –
ask the Homestead Steel strikers

or his would-be assassin,
Berkman. Love too perhaps. At night
he would haunt his collection for hours.

The kettle whistles, the flax
unbends. On the lake, dragonflies,
hover like tiny helicopters.

The wishbone

This is not the saddest story
in the world. But it is sad.
It happened a long time ago.

The six of us were living
in that house on Woodstock Road.
Our friend Sam had dropped out, and he

and Jay were in the room Kael
had had. (Kael claimed he'd once played
with the Tornados but no one

believed him.) That evening
we were all in the kitchen,
watching one of the Bogart films

that ran that spring. *Petrified
Forest*? Not *Maltese Falcon*.
Someone had roasted a chicken,

and Jay got the wishbone. She
was beautiful, blond, direct,
worked in Boots, had a way of flick-

ing her straight hair off her face.
She hooked the wishbone round her
little finger, offered it to Sam,

who hooked it round his little
finger. They pulled. The wishbone
snapped. Sam shut his eyes. You could see

he was wishing really hard.
Opened his eyes, looked at Jay.
'Oh,' he said dully, 'you're still here.'

It's not the saddest story I know,
but it is sad
though it happened a long time ago.

The dentist

Hugh told me the story of the dentist one morning in July 1974. The trays of blackcurrants were tipped onto the conveyor belt, the berries bounced and jiggled, the forklifts came and went, and Hugh and I stood side by side, splitting apples on the trestle table. Hugh was born in Inverness, orphaned, he said, at five months. He had bad teeth, wore a 200-lira piece on a chain round his neck. The heart tattooed on his left forearm carried the legend Mother, Father and a pair of dice. He'd been in the army for nine years, four in Northern Ireland, bought himself out rather than go back. Leant on his axe, showed me the bullet wounds on his chest and leg. The dentist got his nickname because he'd say to his victims, 'We're going to take a ride to see the dentist' before putting a black bag over their heads and shooting them through the mouth. Hugh was part of the detail assigned to capture him. One of them was disguised as a UDA high-up on a much-publicised visit to Belfast. At the Belfast docks, the dentist hi-jacked the taxi but they followed in two jeeps with wirelesses, rammed the taxi out in the country and shot the dentist in the leg when he tried to run away. In one of the jeeps on the way back, the dentist began to boast of his exploits, said he'd only get a few years and then start all over again. The sergeant stopped the jeep and ordered Hugh to give the prisoner his gun. Hugh was puzzled, but did so. The dentist told them to drop their weapons and get out of the jeep. Then he said he would let them go, because it would be a great coup for the dentist. But the sergeant had a weapon concealed under his tunic and shot the dentist several times at point-blank range. The report said that he was shot, trying to escape. Several points in Hugh's story bothered me but I definitely wasn't about to ask him about them as the trays of blackcurrants were tipped onto the conveyor-belt, the berries bounced and jiggled, the forklifts came and went, and, side by side, Hugh and I split apples on the trestle table.

The kingfisher moment

The hot eyes of the horned god:
just that line, marooned in the middle
of a page in red ink

in a 70s notebook – those
distinctive e's of yours, like a bow
drawn tight, those notched arrows.

But what's behind the line? Some
flirtation with fertility cults?
(Pan was pretty big then.)

Some alliterative spasm?
The charm of not knowing exactly
where the stresses should fall?

Was it even your own line?
You could simply have been struck by it
and just written it down.

Not in red, though. Must be yours.
But who or what does it refer to?
I should know; we were close

– more than that, we knew by heart
the Morse code of each other's secret
life; so we used to say.

Probably there were clues, hints,
and I missed the kingfisher moment.
Too late to ask you now.

In Rome With You

'Make love gentle as moonlight':
I wrote that in 1971
in Rome with you, one hot August night.
Make love gentle as moonlight:
well! Back then we called things 'out of sight',
were earnest, idealistic, not much fun.
Make love gentle as moonlight:
I wrote that in 1971.

Your Secret Life 4

(for Jessie)

We walk, talk, laugh in soft November light;
a day to set against the lost years.
No way now to put that misery right;
we walk, talk, laugh in soft November light;
Sometimes we find ourselves quite
overcome and can't hold back the tears,
but still we walk, talk, laugh in soft November light;
a day to set against all the lost years.

Weather

Your beady eyes take everything in.
You don't say but I know you know I know,
especially when you switch to the weather.

In Malaya, a krait slides over your sandal. You read me:
'Pit pat, paddle pat! pit pat, waddle pat!'
Your beady eyes take everything in.

At school, two blue weekly aerogrammes gossip
about picnics on junks, your pinafored pupils,
some soupçon about the Hong Kong weather.

On long summer afternoons over lapsang souchong,
you note my long hair, flares, girlfriends, gay friends:
your beady eyes take everything in.

Once, as I manoeuvre the pushchair, you announce:
'Did you know more couples argue about money
than anything else?' Now I'm never sure whether

to ignore or pre-empt that same old refrain
('Well, we didn't have any rain; that's something'),
not sure how much your beady eyes take in;
you mostly talk of the weather.

Noddy

(in mem Richard Gilmore, 1952–2010)

Noddy: that was what we used to call you
because all that scary first term,
skipping lectures and half-falling in love,
you nearly drove us mad, telling that joke.

One morning bright and early in Toyland
Noddy woke up, got out of bed,
looked out the window and said 'Hello, Sun'
and the Sun said 'Hello, Little Noddy'.

Your fair hair was always carefully brushed.
You wore ties, pink shirts, hush puppies
(I might have invented the hush puppies),
had a raspberries-and-cream complexion.

Then Noddy got dressed, put on his blue hat
with the tinkly bell at the tip
and thought he would go and see his best friend
Big-Ears; so he walked out of his front door.

Once over dinner in the Taj Mahal,
Turl Street – now also gone – you said
what a good housemaster I'd make. I sulked.
I had long hair, beads, played Pink Floyd, read *Oz*.

And whom should Noddy meet but Mr Plod
the Policeman and Mr Plod
said 'Hello, Little Noddy' and Noddy
said 'Hello, Mr Plod' and he walked on.

That first summer vac we met up in Rome,
wandered around the Piazza
Navona, drank martinis, made plans, laughed,
didn't mention that sideways flick of your eyes.

And whom should Noddy meet next but Mr
Golly and Mr Golly said
'Hello, Little Noddy' and Noddy said
'Hello, Mr Golly' and he walked on.

By this point in the joke you'd usually
be spluttering. I wish I'd known
the Mad Man you, still more the later you
who helped in drug and alcohol centres.

And when Noddy reached Big-Ears' toadstool house,
he knocked on the door and Big-Ears
opened the door and Noddy said 'Hello,
Big-Ears' and Big-Ears said 'Fuck off, Noddy!'

I like to think of you best as Thisbe
in that *Midsummer Night's Dream* in Keble
College Gardens we did after Finals.
Every night the audience would crack up

when you lisped 'These lily lips, / This cherry
nose, / These yellow cowslip cheeks', burr-
ing dead Pyramus's lips with a finger.
By the end we were all corpsing, holding back the tears.

Folly House

5:45pm. Guy knocks. He has something very important to say. He is now 'a ball of pure consciousness', and we must all 'derelativise' ourselves to become 'pure consciousness'. He has de-Freudenised himself and understands all his blocks and complexes. He no longer feels any sexual desire. He has also de-Marxised himself and burns a pound note by way of demonstration. He has recognised many 'happy coincidences and omens', such as his 21st birthday falling on Ascension Day. Outside it's getting dark, spring-chilly, the grey river moves under Folly Bridge and past Folly House where Guy walks about, chain-smoking Gauloises, completely assured, hands shaking. He has realised that he has 'impeccable taste' and that Gauloises are the only cigarettes, Bach the only composer, Conran's the only dinner sets. He has a reading list of the Books: Shakespeare, Keats, Isherwood. Everything has led to this moment in time and to him being who he is. When the dons read his philosophy papers in Finals, they will at once see the truth, and the good news will break very soon afterwards.

A Modern Creed

I believe in God the mother, sharer of crystals and echinacea, and in all things organic and gluten-free.

And I believe Jesus was awesome and a very special person, a legend who thought outside the box and wore hemp trousers, and that his life was a journey in which at the death he came to embrace his inner child.

And I believe in blue-sky thinking, de-hiring and moving on. And I believe the reality is and that everything before me is history and old school. And I believe if you avoid sugar, lactose, nicotine and red meat, you will find closure. Have a nice day.

Breton Café, Brandon St

(for Bill)

Hard to hold the thought you died
over a decade ago – another world.
We used to meet here

when it was in other hands.
You liked the slight seediness, rickety chairs,
palpable struggle

to survive, but would enjoy
this later incarnation, not least the chance
to show off your French,

so much more fluent than mine.
You'd have known that *un petit café au lait*
was how to order

a flat white, would have had crêpes,
I'm pretty certain. And I could have told you
about that Sunday

morning a year afterwards
when we scattered your ashes at a small bay
not far from Red Rocks.

We read two of your poems,
tipped the last of you into the sea (some grains
blew back, awkwardly),

had turned, solemn, sad, resigned,
towards the world of croissants, poached eggs, ham,
when we saw Jane's car

was being broken into.
We ran so very slowly across the pebbles,
shouting, waving, sinking,

as the thieves gunned out of sight.
It's a trick, I know, but, if I listen hard enough,
I can just catch your dark laughter.

1970/2015

(with Cath Vidler)

i
A month ago I should have said:
'White roses touched with snow.'
The flakes that hurry past me now
touch roses turned to red.

ii
The roses that said:

flakes
touch
me.

*

Roses,
touched

a month ago
with snow

have turned
past white

to red.

*

I should hurry now.

iii
'Hurry with me,'
said the white roses.

Roses that I should have touched
turned to snow a month ago.

Now past flakes.
Touch that red.

The unmade bed

She sits on the unmade bed, just right
of centre, with something in her hands.
Her dark hair hangs in one long pigtail

down over her right shoulder, the left
her white nightie, décolleté, leaves bare.
Her dropped face, that winsome, downward stare.

On the floor near her naked, crossed feet
are two petite brown boots: one lies flat,
the other toes a blur of paper.

If the scene were contemporary,
she could be holding some flash iPod
or iPhone. She could be listening

to Leonard Cohen, Gillian Welch.
But this almost homely bedsit – wood-
ceilinged, clothes flopped on chair, wash-basin

tucked away in the hearth (what's that shoe
doing on the crumbling mantelpiece?) –
must surely be nineteenth century.

Not English though with that crucifix
hazy behind the open shutter.
Continental? Some provincial

French town, perhaps. A miniature,
that's what she is holding: his picture.
Does the paper – a letter? – announce

he's died or loves another ('Ma chère
Lisette . . .')? Could that black aquascutum,
angled beside the chest of drawers,

have been his? His features swim, she feels
his touch, quickens, finds her mind go numb.
Sunlight slants through the window, catches

the pretty, floral bedspread, picks out
a painting above it on the wall.
Shadows. Steps. A locked embrace. She wears

a blue dress, he a red cape, jaunty
plume in his cap. She is leaning back
to receive a last, quick, lunging kiss.

This is how it should have, should have, been.
Not here, alone on an unmade bed
in this room, bright, sad, slightly shabby.

Wain with an 'I'

Did you once see John Wain plain?
Yes, Wain with an 'I', that is –
not the gun-toting cowpoke who rode

our childhood's pastoral range
(still does on bad nights), reading
smoke signals at a glance, ornery

honest with his drawled 'Howdy'.
No, the John Wain who wrote – you
know, it's still sometimes seen as the first

angry young man novel.
Before Amis's *Lucky Jim*
(though that's a better novel by far).

Give up? It's *Hurry On Down*.
Anyway, Wain was living
near the canal. Wolvercote, was it?

And Dave and I interviewed
him for a magazine called
OSAC which nobody read

because it was free (this was
1973). Wain
was a dumpy, affable chap, wore

a Bob Dylan cap, made us
good coffee, didn't seem put out
that we knew nothing about his work.

He was writing the poems
for *Feng*. I bought it later.
At the time, he looked antique, someone

from a lost world, out of place
in ours. Only forty-eight,
many years younger than I am now.

Soon to become professor
of poetry – or was he
that already? Did we know or care?

He was keen on David Jones,
said his poems would endure.
Also that they'd set *Hurry On Down*

for English A Level.
He said this in a pleased way.
We made no comment, feeling mildly

superior to writers
who cared about money, fame.
'Selling out' we called it, not having

anything ourselves to sell
out for but quietly certain,
like John Wayne, that we wouldn't anyway.

Room

Here's the room at the top of the house,
just as cold as it often was; to the left
against the wall the bed in which
you had bronchitis and read Barbara Pym;

and here the desk on which you marked
twenty-five essays on bad sex in *The Waste Land* –
as if there could be anything like a good fuck
in those dismal interiors or narrow canoes.

Here's the window still letting in sky
the colour of the corduroy shorts you wore
at that imaginary homeland, school – no,
wrong turning, false trail. Go back

to the desk, the copy of Empson's poems
with the yellow dustjacket: *It is the poems*
you have lost, the ills / From missing dates –
the downstairs world of daleks, laughter,

Blondie, half-shut off, trying out
the emotional red shift of a villanelle,
lines bending, warping, on each return.
Here's the room at the top of the house.

Second chances

The thing with second chances
so much depends upon luck.
You might pretend you're in some updated

Regency novel, all smart
phones, range rovers, wit, lattes,
even sex. Dream on. You're no 'only Anne',

although, come to that, doesn't luck
(the pen dealing a marked deck –
Lyme Regis, Louisa's fall on the Cobb)

determine the happily
ever after? And you know
you know that's not how these things really go.

Yet, for you, somehow they did.
You were, in the middle way,
mire-deep in misery, sinking, clutching.

And then, suddenly, dry land,
new life, the ever whatever.
It wasn't deserved, wasn't virtue rewarded.

No imaginary friend
didn't, like, miraculously
intervene or anything; no sirree.

It didn't make sense, and still doesn't.
But you took the chance when it came
again, trusted love not persuasion.

About (1980/2004/2014)

Love, we knew, was what it was about;
that, and what we called 'the drift'.
It was easy to believe and not to doubt.

Get the loot, don't be slow, we're gonna catch a trout;
open roads; orchards of promise; how we *If*-ed
love's magic roundabout.

Neither words nor tears could relieve the drought;
the lute's cracked tune required the rift.
It was easy to believe and not to doubt.

Time, we mused, was always running out;
don't look back: lines jump, merge and shift.
Ah, the pursuit of love and all that was about.

Old friends die; others grow devout;
harder now to think life a gift.
It was easy to believe and not to doubt.

Now questions riddle this read-out;
fog forms and will not lift.
Love, we knew, was what it was about;
it was easy to believe and not to doubt.

from *Winter Eyes*

Song

i
The song feels like singing,
looks out the window:

clouds glued to the sky,
harbour slate-grey,
hills like collapsed elephants.

There's food stuck to the highchair,
a plastic spoon on the floor.
The cat stares up in awe at the fridge.

The song opens its mouth,
but seems to have forgotten the words.

ii
The song wakes up.
It's dark.

Someone is crying.
The morepork in the ngaio

shakes out its slow spondee:
more pork more pork more pork.

Back in the dream a line
of faces passes the window.

Each face smiles, lifts
its lips to show large teeth.

iii

The song sits at the window, humming
ever so softly, tapping

a rhythm on the table-edge, watching
the harbour slowly losing

colour. At the very far end
of the harbour slightly up to the right,

a zip of lights marks the hill
over to Wainuiomata. If that zip

could be unzipped, thinks the song,
the whole world might change.

iv

The song strokes the past
like a boa, like some fur muff
or woollen shawl,

but the past is not soft at all;
it's rough to the touch,
sharp as broken glass.

v

The song longs to sing in tune.
The song longs to be in tune.

The black dog comes whenever
the song whistles, wagging its tail.

The black dog waits for the song's whistle.
The black dog wants a long walk.

vi

The song croons 'Here Comes the Night'
very quietly. Meanwhile the baby
spoons its porridge into a moon.

The black dog leads the song
down long, unlovely streets.
The night is slowly eating the moon.

At Shimla

(for Jan and Harish)

Here we sit at an oval table,
inset with green push-button mics,
holding forth on Kipling

in what was once the Small Drawing-Room
of the Viceregal Lodge, that testament
to colonial camp,

but which now houses the Indian
Institute of Advanced Study. We talk
of soul murder, Southsea,

cultural ambivalence in *Kim*,
hostipality in 'The Man Who Was',
cross-currents in 'Naboth'.

Above the doors, full-cream cornices,
surmount scroll brackets. Higher still, Gandhi
Nehru, Tagore, Naidu –

'Wordsworth in a sari' (Gosse) – smile down
from gold, linen-fold walls at Kipling's gaffes,
how story's now turned fact

and Mowgli really does have a cave
in Seoni. Spurts of laughter. Questions.
Someone runs out of time.

Through the square of window a glimpse
of country house garden, kempt lawn, rumour
of Himalayan snow

– no, I invented the snow, but not
the delphiniums on the mantelpiece,
so delicate and blue.

How much did Kipling know about drugs?
Did Lockwood have an Indian mistress?
The light begins to fail.

Love

(for Paula)

Iris Murdoch's said
to have said that love was taking
the other one for granted.

Sounds all wrong somehow;
but it's not that different from Donne's
'Which watch not one another

out of fear' – a line
Evelyn, after the fall, would give
as his ideal of love.

Then there's Brasch, his wish
for 'someone to share the world with'.
You could go for that now, couldn't you?

14A Esmonde Road

(for Tim and Deb)

Just as Tim said, you could blink
and miss it; but, close up, a partially
obscured board claims that this pale-green

jut of fibrolite is where New Zealand literature
had its origins. Something like that. No sign
now of the famous hole in the hedge

would-be protégés would push through
with such hopes or the army hut at the back
where Frame wrote *Owls Do Cry*.

But on this mild late August morning
finches and wax-eyes fidget and flicker
in the rātā and the loquat, and on the thin

ribbon of grass to the right, a large white
rabbit with chocolate ears rolls slowly
to its feet and decadently hops under the fence.

On Not Meeting Auden

And did you once see Auden plain?
Well, no, though I could have any time
in late '72, early '73.

Sightings were reported daily
on the Broad and High: 'He was wearing
slippers, man!' 'He was holding plastic shopping bags.'

He would hang out in the café
in St Aldates, down from Carfax Tower
(where helmeted boys hammer out the quarter-hours),

but we never went: too Christian.
Besides, old fart with a ruined face,
what could he tell us about life, about poetry –

anything? We had beads, long hair,
Afghans and grants, ideals and flares.
We hitched to Greece, got *Crow*, got stoned, got the lyrics

of *Ziggy Stardust*, *Transformer*.
We knew exactly what Dylan meant
by that line: 'I didn't realise how young you were.'

Picnic

My mother folds, refolds
the paper napkins she hoards
from the Home. Her smile is polite,

expectant, her swollen
legs hidden in blue trousers,
her hair could do with a good brush.

She bites at the cheese scone
I've buttered and quartered, chews
slowly. 'Yesterday,' she begins,

'it was whurr-whurr-whurr.' Stops.
'It was,' I say. 'But today
it's calm and bright.' 'Yes,' she agrees,

grudgingly. 'Yesterday,
whurr-whurr-whurr.' A cruise ship's in.
The café is full of voices

full of money, mostly
American, but also
Australian, European.

A zoo of zimmer-frames,
bottoms that shouldn't wear jeans
much less shorts. My mother watches

a sparrow watching her scone.
I pour her tea, milk in first.
'Yesterday,' she says, 'whurr-whurr-whurr.'

Fitz-Greene Halleck (1790–1867)

(for Roger)

Your statue sits in Central Park
together with Shakespeare and Burns and Scott.
Swathed, cross-legged, mutton-chop-whiskered,
you stare into silence. From your right hand
dangles a pen like a .45.
10,000 saw the dedication.

You belonged to the Knickerbocker
Group. You were admired by Dickens, were dubbed
'the American Byron', though
Poe regarded your 'Fanny' as 'little
less than torture'. Your friend, Joseph Drake,
you thought 'perhaps the handsomest man

in New York', and called his marriage:
'a sacrifice at the shrine of Hymen'.
He died young, soon after, tb.
His widow hoped to marry you, the witch.
Alnwick Castle, with Other Poems
pub. 1827 made your name.

You worked for John Jacob Astor,
were a trustee of what later became
the New York Public Library,
retired to Guildford, lived with your sister.
Your last words, so they say, were: 'Marie,
hand me my pantaloons, if you please.'

Now you're head of the oubliette
near Kipling's 'limbo of lost endeavour
where all the characters go', greet
each newcomer with that New England charm:

'Robert, welcome. Rosamund. *Mark*!'
Your statue sits in Central Park.

Margravine Cemetery, Barons Court

(for Shane and John)

Margravine, a sort of countess,
wife of the keeper of lands between.

Mar, mare, ravine, ravin, raven,
grave, marge, margin, margarine,
rave, also gave, grain, gain, grin . . .

Here in this fine and public space,
the grey squirrels and the pigeons rule.

One squirrel runs up
an old woman's leg,
takes the nut from her hand.

'You cheeky,' she says. Her creased face.
A child wakes, cries, is lifted up, soothed.

This grave is a-tilt
as though the earth moved:
Agnes. Something. *Faithful . . .*

Red and yellow leaves steering down
the soft October afternoon.

Accident

Looking back nearly forty years, the ironies flash out so clearly. First, the misfire of a meeting in that clothes shop in High St Ken; we were both there but failed to see each other. Then the crash in South London. Late at night, the car slid on the slippery road. I remember from the back (no seatbelts) thinking as we headed for the wall, so this is it. Then I went under the seat, knocked out, came to, sirens, lights, dark. Woke up in Lewisham Hospital with a headache and a bashed hip. The white male patients were horrible to the black female nurses. Shane rescued me. He was helping you move flat. I came along hobbling on a stick. You invited me out to a Chinese restaurant off Leicester Square. There was something about your face, that hawk look, the full stare. There.

Indirect Popcorn 2

This agreeably battered and foxed copy
of *The Pill Versus the Springhill Mine Disaster*

(Jonathan Cape, 1970) was given to me
by the painter Karl Maughan. According

to the flyleaf, it had previously belonged
to Peggy Dunstan, whose capital D resembles

a distant sail suddenly filled by the wind.
Alongside is the price $14.

I'd vaguely assumed that no one read Brautigan now,
that he had disappeared into some time-warp,

where they still roll up to *Hangman's Beautiful Daughter*,
say 'trippy tray', lounge with the shine of youth.

But when I asked Karl's wife Emily, who's a novelist
and teaches creative writing, she said that some

of her students read Brautigan and particularly like
'The Revenge of the Lawn' and *Trout Fishing in America*.

Phil, an Aussie friend in Hong Kong, was a fan
of *The Hawkline Monster: A Gothic Western*,

used to read out bits while the sun,
a bloated leech, slid behind Lion Rock.

On page 75 of this battered, foxed copy
of *The Pill Versus the Springhill Mine Disaster*

is a seven-line poem called 'Indirect Popcorn'
and, underneath, written slantwise in black ink:

John,
Just a little
thing you'll
find sometime.
I hope you're
happy
Ina
with love

Sansibar oder der letzte Grund

This soft winter Wellington morning
the harbour throws up its shield,
molten-gold. I know, bit fancy,

but up in some sweltering classroom
c. 1966,
a galaxy far, far away,

'Paint It Black' and 'See Emily Play'
spool a continuous loop,
and 'Prew' Willey nudges us through

Sansibar oder der letzte Grund.
In one scene, Judith – Jewish,
on the run – enters a café.

The owner hints that he might help her
if she stays till closing time.
He has a *Lampiongesicht.*

'And what will they do then, sir?' we ask,
agog at what he might say.
'O je, Jungen! What they will do

is the washing up.' The next two years,
'doing the washing up' meant
only one thing, our private code.

Back in the novel, we learn Gregor
(who'll effect Judith's escape)
lost his belief in communism

when, one evening on manoeuvres
near Tarasovka, he saw
the lake threw up its golden shield

and realised that changed everything,
now nothing would fit again.
Some years later, 'Prew' was required

to take early retirement. He'd asked
a boy to do the washing up.
The harbour has turned pewter grey.

There's activity on Somes Island
– pā, then quarantine station,
detention centre. Von Zedlitz

may've been interned there in WWI.
The wind's picked up; time to move.
Things look different through winter eyes.

from Poems for Max (1970–2014)

Remembering

I remember you were mad about Dylan, the Stones, the Who,
Billy Bragg.

I remember hearing how on a long walk at Thorpeness you sat on
Shane's shoulders the whole way, reading *Asterix* and never once
looked up.

I remember you made one of your brothers a birthday cake, still
known as 'the earthquake'.

I remember you and reality became estranged.

I remember that single, patient, painfully correct fifty you scored
at Benburn Park.

I remember hearing how in Lancaster you got your head stuck
between some railings and it took hours to release you.

I remember writing you that poem when they threw iceballs at
you in the playground and you got caught for throwing them too.

I remember those pictures you drew, full of soldiers and planes
and hidden stories.

I remember your handwriting, wandering, wavering, lurching off
the page, 'diabetic as a newt'.

I remember Brian telling me you woke up once in his flat in
Rome and, before you opened your eyes, you said: 'What Tony
Blair has to realise is . . .'

I remember you asking me, using the window over my left shoulder as a mirror: 'You don't think my head's too small, do you?'

I remember, when I first knew you, you still said 'pule' and 'skule'.

I remember the hours you spent teaching yourself to catch, throwing a tennis ball against the wall of the flat: thud, thud, thud.

Good Looks

Here you are again; your handwriting, at least.
In my copy of *Good Looks*, page twelve, you've underlined

in pencil: *The bodies are weapons, someone will die of them.*
Did you just think it a good line? What did it mean to you

twenty-plus years ago? Against *You must abandon
your pain, it is someone else's* (also underlined),

you've written *a bit like 1965–6 Dylan*
– as it is. There was a time, a long time,

I'd have rubbed it out as I started to in my Seamus Heaney
Selected Poems. But now all's past amend, let the faint,

wavering marks stand, as though you'd just written them
– you're smoking, of course, flicking ash, just like I do,

excited at your own thought, at the act of trespass,
still quick with promise, still friends with possibility.

Making Strange 2

I took you to the cricket today
– meant to at least, inside my copy
of *Station Island* which I assumed
you'd annotated, just as you did
my other Heaneys those years ago.

Earlier in Vic Books with flat whites,
Marco and Ross discussed 'Making Strange',
agreed that it was Heaney's father
'bewildered' in the field 'in the tubs
of his wellingtons', Louis Simpson

the one with 'travelled intelligence'
brought to meet him. (They were unconvinced
by my suggestion both were Heaney:
the stay-at home, the seasoned poet.)
Ross, at some point, said for anyone

Irish 'making strange' would call to mind
a child being awkward with adults.
At the Basin, it was hot, the game
long gone. Lyon was looping them up,
Southee hitting sixes, holing out.

I reread the poem, rinsed the rest
of the book, certain that somewhere
I'd come across your spidery script.
But if you'd ever been there, you'd left
no sign, nothing to make the loss less strange.

Grief Limericks

1

I once had a stepson called Max.
As a child, he could rarely relax.
The other kids kicked him;
he was a natural victim.
I once had a stepson called Max.

2

I once had a stepson called Max,
liked Gunn and *Blood on the Tracks*.
But things were askew,
tangled in blue.
I once had a stepson called Max.

3

I once had a stepson called Max
with needs as tender as wax.
When I left his mother,
he saw me as other.
I once had a stepson called Max.

4

I once had a stepson called Max
whose memories turned into tacks.
Love inside out
helps hatred to sprout.
I once had a stepson called Max.

5

I once had a stepson called Max
with a head full of cricketing facts,
who one winter's day

I once had a stepson called Max.

At Lake Rotoma

Out there, all this hot, bright morning,
the tūī working the flax,
white bibs bobbing up and down.

In here, it's cooler and dimmer,
deep in my *English Auden*,
suddenly your ghost again.

Beside the lines *your private lust*
Something to do with violence
and the poor, in that wonky

script of yours you've written the word:
(homosexuality).
I see you, eighteen, smoking,

excitedly deciphering
the code – why those brackets, though?
I did ask you once, somewhere

in Courtenay Place, if you were gay.
You said no; so let it drop.
In any case, who cares now?

Sex wasn't your problem although love
may have been, or lack of it
a long way back. This sets off

a further echo: 'Love Again',
that dismaying semi-striptease.
I look it up, realise

Larkin simply lifted the line
Something to do with violence
straight from the Auden poem

– just the kind of pickpocketing
you were good at spotting, still
hopeful, before the madness.

Or so I choose to think. A blind
opening of no earthly use
to you, Auden or Larkin.

Out there, the tūī work the flax,
their beaks orange with pollen,
feathers the blue-black of a bruise.

Oxford: A Tritina

'The mental onanism of unrecorded thought'
is not the sort of line you
often hear (or a condition many writers are prone to). It was said
   one evening by

my bearded roommate, who by
the fifth week of term had become the College stud. (I thought
the noises from next door would drive me mad.) You

can tire of making tea for pretty girls quite uninterested in you,
who haven't grasped his absence means goodbye
and whom in the dawn you've overheard whisper the thought:

'I thought you might be changed by love.'

Masks

Who in these late and dangerous days
would walk abroad without a mask?
In faded red ink. Then, *Venice, '72.*

What on earth were the lines supposed to
mean? That life was a cross between *Strange Days*
and *The Duchess of Malfi*: some scary, carnival masque?

Maybe. Everyone then did wear a mask
or so it seemed, and could change it, too:
a mask for the nights, a mask for the days.

In those days there seemed so much to mask up to.

That Summer

I worked shifts in a Ribena factory that summer
Clare made my heart a great wound.
All I wanted was to be off and roam.

Hitching then was the best way to roam,
so I hitched round Greece that summer,
my thumb and I and the wound.

Eventually of course the wound
closed up. I got robbed, lost the urge to roam,
took the ferry to Italy late that summer.

Which is how, that summer, I wound up meeting Brian in Rome.

Spring

Cape daisies mauve the hills, give a spring
to the spirit my mother beside me will not hold
onto, any more than the rhododendron's pink –

'Oh lovely!' She too was once in the pink,
a student in the black-out, and it's spring,
and she's in love's stranglehold,

and hears someone play 'Greensleeves' from the hold
of the dark, making her face go pink
and her heart spring,

and spring hold out its bright, pink cone.

Good Friday 2017, driving north

(for Belinda)

Annunciation lighting strobes
the late, autumn afternoon, picks out

wet paddocks, a hawk stooping, cows,
full-grown lambs, a donkey, sheep, sheep, sheep.

'Wouldn't It Be Nice'; 'Sloop John B'.
Semaphore of leaves, crimson and gold.

Eketāhuna already:
three small, white crosses by the golf course.

Spermatozoa rain-drops squirm
on the windscreen, up down, up down.

'Look,' you say, 'rainbow on the right'
– thick and delicious as marble-cake.

High on the hills in tricksy light,
wind turbines spin like Catherine Wheels.

Room 10

You look asleep when I tiptoe in
but your eyes flick open as I pull

a chair across. I reach for your hand,
your fingers tissue-soft, stroking mine.

The wind tugs the curtain through the door
which leads onto the inner courtyard.

The sunlight reminds me suddenly
of your garden, sitting on the lawn.

It's hot. You're drinking lapsang souchong,
trying, that way you have, to find out

whether I'm serious about S,
whom neither of us names. It's quiet.

I light a cigarette to evade
further questions. You sip your tea.

But now you're mumbling something, something.
Then, and quite distinctly: 'It's lovely.'

'It's all right,' I say. 'It's all right.'
Your fingers, tissue-soft, stroke mine.

The Galton Case

In Christopher Fowler's *Book of Forgotten Authors*, Margaret Millar receives several pages. Previously I'd only come across her through a line in a Richard Thompson song called 'Cold Kisses' in which the rather creepy protagonist, after checking his absent girlfriend's drawers for evidence of his past rivals, and finding plenty of it, has, on her return, his head 'buried' in a 'Margaret Millar mystery'. (Thompson in later versions changed the line to a 'Dan Brown mystery'.) Fowler mentions that Millar was married to Ross MacDonald and that the marriage was 'feisty'. Perhaps this explains that line on page 155 of his *Black Money*. MacDonald's plots are straight out of the house of Atreus, the solution to a crime in the present always lies, it turns out, in an unsolved family crime in the past. MacDonald is one of those writers, Kipling is another, who likes to smuggle in something literary. At the end of *The Galton Case*, for instance, Lew Archer has worked out what happened in both the present and the past. Several people have died, and we're left with Lew, the young man who really is the heir to the fortune, after all, and not a fake, his loyal girlfriend and his mother, all now free but still seemingly trapped in 'the gorgon past'. And then 'a single bird raised its voice for a few notes, then fell into abashed silence'. The bird starts again, and they listen ('Even the dead man seemed to be listening'). And there we are pitched vertiginously right in the middle of Emily Dickinson's '"Hope" is the thing with feathers': 'And sweetest – in the Gale – is heard – / And sore must be the storm – / That could abash the little Bird / That kept so many warm –'. But who reads Ross MacDonald either?

Napier, Christmas 2017

Shock your Mum. Come to Church.
says the sign. Fudged hills, jacarandas, pink silk trees.
Many Bargains in store. Buddha's conditions apply.

Poppy surfs the slapping waves; pebbles scramble underfoot.
Jack hits Tom over the fence.
Shock your Mum. Come to Church.

Mother, I think, went mostly for the music,
father because he was a soldier and a Christian.
Many Bargains in store. Buddha's conditions apply.

Which conditions don't seem that different from the Beatitudes,
though the specials vary, also the rewards and punishments.
Shock your Mum. Come to Church.

Here's the lightning, then the thunder, then Casey,
laughing, splish-sploshing in the rain.
Many Bargains in store. Buddha's conditions apply.

The first hawk is quartering the vines.
The future overtakes us somewhere near Ongaonga.
Shock your Mum. Come to Church.
Many Bargains in store. Buddha's conditions apply.

Oddly Like a Bee

Today you're not in your room
but in the common room.

A newspaper is open on the table,
Jacinda Ardern the headline.

You wouldn't have voted for her.
'She should wear her hair up,'

I can hear your old self say.
I put my white sunglasses on the table

and place my right hand in yours.
You stroke my fingers, are puzzled

by the rectangular silver ring. 'Clare
gave me that in 1970,' I say.

'I always wear it.' (I had her name
inscribed, then – rightly – thinking

she'd find that vulgar, had it erased.
She married her tutor, had two daughters,

died years ago, angry with God.)
My mother's given up on the ring

and has picked up my sunglasses.
She turns them over and over

in her knobbly fingers, and very carefully
puts them on. They make her look

oddly like a bee. When I wheel her into lunch,
kiss her goodbye, she's still wearing them.

Hump-backed Moon

This 'thinly plotted' pantomime
must always end too soon.
There'll be time, we say; there'll be time
to rewrite our part in the pantomime
to embrace the promise of the approaching rhyme
to feed our gaze on this hump-backed moon
eerily rising on this pantomime,
which must always end too soon.

New Poems

Bits and pieces #3

These bits and pieces don't fit;
so all you can do is make it up.

This patch of blue might be sky,
but, just as easily, deep water.

This bit could be a hill twinked
in cloud; this a broken stump; and this

the torn cover of a book.
Mostly, though, it's a tombola stall

of what look like body parts:
a tooth, a knee, what could be an eye

or something else entirely.
This might be red hair, this undergrowth.

Quite a few of the pieces
seem consistent with an old crash site.

Ginny's Garden

(for Ginny Sullivan, 1950–2017)

In the high firs magpies quardle-oodle.
Down here it's warm under the overhang,

looking out across the lawn Karen says she cut
two weeks ago, now already thick, clumpy.

In the paddock Friendly, the seven-year-old ewe
which you couldn't bear to send to the butcher,

maas by the fence for kale and attention.
The veggies you planted have gone mad:

rampant marrows; tomatoes big as butternuts;
cabbage whites all over the basil.

In the Pears' Soap poster in the bathroom,
one small girl shows another the wonder of bubbles.

Last day

The *Dom Post* nine-letter Target word
is 'Purgatory'. I hold

your hand. The veins are thick, dark rivers.
Your mouth a wide O;

your breath, quick, snatching at air.
It's much too warm in here.

You would hate me to see you like this:
so gaunt, so vulnerable.

This morning, as I climbed the steps,
a parakeet, red waistcoat,

yellow stomacher, was piping its heart out.
'Her heart's tired,' the doctor says.

My fingers sting with pins and needles.
Your face has sunk to bone.

The Assassination of St Peter Martyr
(for Jan)

Here we are in the National Gallery
this autumn afternoon, carried by the crowd
past Saint Sebastians, madonnas with child,

crucifixions to this Bellini, a bit
murky, and a painting neither of us knows.
It's not instantly obvious which friar

(both are Dominican, both under attack)
is the saint, but, presumably, not the one
bottom left, a dagger sticking in his chest.

Must be the other, centre stage, stretching
away from the assassin with the raised axe.
The story goes that St Peter, also known

as Peter of Verona, is reciting
the opening of the creed: *Credo in Deum*.
The blow from that axe will cut off his head.

Pope Gregory IX made him General
Inquisitor, so he'd have known about pain.
(His assassin, Carino of Balsamo,

was hired by Cathars, heretics whom Peter
regularly preached against and converted,
though, it's said, he was brought up Cathar himself.)

'Fastest canonisation in history',
apparently: just eleven months later.
In the painting, seemingly oblivious

to the murder, men chop down trees, a shepherd
sits by a lamb, light gilds a distant city.
But now we're outside again, Trafalgar Square;

the crowd is dissolving in the darkling air.
Time for goodbyes, to check mobiles, to return
to our world of assassinations, fake news.

Arguments for religion

Your soul in constant peril. The drama
of every action quick with consequence.
It's not hard to see the appeal.

Imagine sleeping with your friend's wife or husband
not just a terrible betrayal but a mortal sin.
Your soul in constant peril. The drama.

Imagine God and the Devil equally
concerned with your every thought, word and deed.
It's not hard to see the appeal.

Imagine the roads to Damascus, struggles, epiphanies,
vigils in your very own dark night.
Your soul in constant peril. The drama.

Are you a sadist? A masochist?
Physical pain, spiritual suffering, guaranteed.
It's not hard to see the appeal.

Social media, imperial nostalgia, dark money, fake news,
measuring out your life with coffee-spoons.
Your soul in constant peril. The drama.
It's not hard to see the appeal.

Napier

(for Jessie)

This café, formerly known as Ujazi
(meaning 'supply' or 'drink' in Swahili),

is one you and I discovered twenty years ago. It's now
called Café Tennyson after the street it's on,

which sets up far less exotic associations.
Hard to imagine Tennyson coffee-housing here,

his head wreathed in clouds of shag tobacco,
intoning in his broad Norfolk accent.

Easier to think of Napier itself, named after
the sender of that one-word message: *Peccavi.*

(Mr Maurice, glaring through his pince-nez,
explicated the pun with savage relish –

wrongly, as it turns out. The major-general did annexe
Sindh, but it was Catherine Winkworth who made up the pun.)

Which conveniently leaves out Ahuriri, meaning (perhaps)
'a fence to catch fish' or 'a barrier to prevent flooding'.

The past's a mosaic so complicated only the foolish
would try to simplify it. The coffee's still good though.

The writing life

You want to write.
You want to be published.
You want to be read.

You want 'fit audience though few'.
You want to be reviewed.
You want to write.

You want to win prizes.
You want to be anthologised.
You want to be read.

You want to be taught in schools and at uni.
You want books written about you.
You want to write.

You want to be translated.
You want other writers to admire your work.
You want to be read.

You want eulogies and elegies at your death.
You want to be remembered forever.
You want to write.
You want to be read.

Author's Note

How poets first encounter poetry and start to write it has always fascinated me, and compiling this *Selected Poems* seems an adequate excuse for briefly offering my own account.

The turning point was a poetry-writing weekend at the Lancaster Arts Festival in my late twenties, and having children.

At prep school, we had learnt by heart poems like John Masefield's 'Cargoes', Alfred Noyes's 'The Highwayman' and Kipling's 'Gunga Din', and had to stand up in class and recite them the following day. This was nerve-racking, but I still know the poems. Occasionally we had to write a poem, which was equally nerve-racking. (The precocious boy who not only accurately translated the homework extract from Ovid's 'Tristia' but turned it into verse was universally loathed.) At secondary school I became besotted with Keats and T.S. Eliot, and produced alliteration-drenched, would-be-witty lines in what I thought was free verse.

Oxford was worse. The English curriculum was a whistle-stop tour of the greatest literary hits from Anglo–Saxon to Auden – wonderful in its way, but deeply intimidating for anyone trying to write their own poems (unless you were James Fenton or Andrew Motion, already embryonic stars). My friends and I were terrified of being thought 'young' or 'normal', and wanted our lives to be as weird and intense as the music we so obsessively listened to: 'Desolation Row', 'Heroin', 'White Rabbit', 'Bird on a Wire', 'Big Yellow Taxi', 'In the Court of the Crimson King', 'After the Gold Rush', 'Riders on the Storm'. Dylan, Mitchell, Morrison seemed in their way as lyrically, emotionally and intellectually out of reach as Donne, Marvell, Blake, and more urgent. During my first job (in Hong Kong), I had a fantasy of writing song lyrics for a cult band.

Back in England, the poetry weekend. This was run by Gavin Ewart. He's mostly forgotten now, but he had his moment in the sun. Like Auden, he used poetic form as a starter motor and turned out everything from villanelles to clerihews, from prose poems to McGonagallesque doggerel. The first day he had us write haiku, limericks and one-line poems. One man stormed out, shouting this wasn't poetry, but for me it was a revelation. I was still very hung up on Romantic notions of having to be in the creative mood, sometimes 'suitably enhanced', and found trying out the forms enormously liberating – and fun. I was rather pleased with my limerick:

'Writing limericks is all very well,'
said Milton to Andrew Marvell;
'but I should have thought
five lines was too short
for my epic of heaven and hell.'

The second day, we workshopped poems we'd sent in advance. (Mine was 'Peking History Lesson 1977', the first poem in this collection.) Ewart was very firm about line endings (not weak words like 'a', 'of' or 'the') and about not being lazy with rhyme, if you used it: every word had to earn its keep. That weekend helped me to be less earnest about poetry, but also to take the writing of it more seriously.

This shift coincided with having children, and I would Blu-Tack drafts of poems to the walls and think about them as I walked around, holding unsleeping babies. Sometimes the poems were about my children. Becoming a parent not only made a huge difference to me as a person, but also gradually to the poems I was beginning to write, like 'Your Secret Life', about my daughter Jessie. Everyone finds their own way, but that was mine.

—H.R.

Notes

29–32: These four 'found' sonnets are part of a set of fourteen I extracted in 1986 from a copy which I still have of Sir Apirana Ngata's *Maori Grammar & Conversation With Vocabulary* (Sixth Printing Revised and Enlarged by W.W. Bird, published by Whitcombe & Tombs, price 3/9d, no publication date). I subsequently discovered through A.G. Bagnall's New Zealand National Bibliography that the edition I had been using should have described itself as the ninth printing and that it was published in 1948. Not only that, but Sir Apirana Ngata's name was first associated with editions of the grammar book from 1901, and he was not the first compiler as I had initially imagined. The original compiler was Sister Mary Joseph Aubert, who published the first version of the grammar in 1885 under the initials 'S.A.' and with the title *New And Complete Manual of Maori Conversation With A Complete Vocabulary*. So, a complex and entangled publication history.

All the sentences and questions reproduced in the poems and arranged into different sonnet shapes are exactly as they appeared with their Māori counterparts not only in the Ngata version but (with one exception not in this selection) in Sister Aubert's original text. The nature of those sentences and questions seemed to me thirty-five years ago and seem to me now to offer some extraordinary, often dismaying, glimpses into late nineteenth-century Aotearoa New Zealand society, its mores and its assumptions.

76: G.S. Fraser, the Scottish poet and critic, died in 1980. In one of his last poems, 'Older', he cast himself as a kind of latter-day Polonius figure. 'Polonius: Old Poet', written while George was still alive, was intended as a reply to 'Older'. The other two Polonius poems were written shortly after his death.

143: The triolet is one of those French forms with repeating lines that date back to medieval times. It was introduced into English in the late nineteenth century. The pattern is relatively simple: eight lines with two rhyme sounds, in which lines 1–2 are repeated as lines 7–8, and line 1 is also repeated as line 4. So, the triolet is a bit like a stunted villanelle, but whereas there are a number of well-known villanelles in English (for instance, Dylan Thomas's 'Do Not Go Gentle Into That Good Night', William Empson's 'Missing Dates', Elizabeth Bishop's 'One Art', Derek Mahon's 'Antarctica' – and, locally, Jenny Bornholdt's 'Villanelle' and Bill Manhire's 'Luck: A Villanelle'), there are no equally well-known triolets, with the possible exception of Thomas Hardy's 'How Great My Grief'. Frances Stillman in her invaluable *The Poet's Manual and Rhyming Dictionary* (1966) gives the probable reason for this neglect: 'The triolet was originally used as a vehicle for serious poetry, but it is now considered a light form that should not be required to carry too deep or complicated a meaning.' That the English poet Wendy Cope included several triolets in *Family Values* (2011) seems to bear out Stillman's claim. Or does it? Cope was irritated by reviewers who dismissed her witty first book, *Making Cocoa for Kingsley Amis* (1986), as 'light verse' (as though 'light' necessarily means 'slight'), and pointedly called her second collection *Serious Concerns*. Some of the triolets in *Family Values* are funny but by no means all, and no one would call Hardy's 'How Great My Grief' 'light'. Which suggests the triolet still offers opportunities for poets not allergic to form.

I began writing triolets in October 2012 after the Australian poet Cath Vidler confessed an addiction to the form and encouraged me to try it. I soon found that, like the villanelle, the restrictions and repetitions of the triolet can lead to writing poems not merely playfully or self-consciously ingenious (nothing wrong with that of course) but poems embodying confinement and the inability to break out of particular cycles of thought, feeling and behaviour. As with the sonnet and the villanelle, it is also possible to push the form of the triolet in various ways, including emptying out the rhyme altogether and preserving the exo-skeletal shape.

154: 'The unmade bed' began as an unseen ekphrastic exercise using Gerolamo Induno's painting *Risorgimento*.

178: The novel *Sansibar oder der letzte Grund* by Alfred Andersch really exists.

184: The 'grief limerick' is a term coined by Nick Ascroft and poignantly demonstrated in his 'Five Limericks on Grief' (*Back with the Human Condition*, 2016). This gave me the cue for my poem 'Grief Limericks'.

187–190: It was Cath Vidler who kindly encouraged me to try the tritina, just as in 2012 she encouraged me to try the triolet. Tritina: it sounds as though it should be an old poetic form, but in fact it was invented quite recently by the American poet Marie Ponsot, who neatly described it as 'the square root of the sestina'. The form's most obvious challenges are those of compression, fluidity and repetition (only ten lines, with three end-words redeployed in a set order). The results are I hope more than five-finger exercises.

Index of Titles

Index of First Lines